How to Plan &
Write Your Book

A Rural Author's Guide

Sarah Walkerden

The Rural
Publishing Company

The Rural Publishing Company

First published by The Rural Publishing Company.

Revised edition 2025.

Copyright © 2022 Sarah Walkerden

eBook: 978-0-6484431-4-8
Print: 978-0-6484431-5-5

Cover Design: The Rural Publishing Company
Layout & Typesetting: The Rural Publishing Company

The Rural Publishing Company
Website: https://theruralpublishingcompany.com.au
Email: hello@theruralpublishingcompany.com.au

Contents

Introduction

Books can be written for a range of different purposes in a wide variety of styles. And what motivates you as a potential author could be vastly different to what might motivate someone else.

However, regardless of the type of book, the purpose and motivation behind that book, or the style – there is one key thing that ALL authors have in common.

The need to share a story.

Whether that's a fictional story, or a piece of information – if you're reading this book, there's a really good chance that something inside you is whispering to you that you need to share something important to a group of people who matter.

And yet too few people actually get around to writing and publishing their book.

Far too many manuscripts get started and never finished – or they get finished but never published. Merely gathering dust in a desk drawer or in a hidden folder on a computer.

Which is a great, great shame for the rest of us.

Because no matter how saturated you might feel the market is with your type of book – there's EVERY chance that there is someone out there in the world who WANTS and NEEDS to hear it from YOU!

Only you can write like you (with the exception of a talented ghost writer!).

Only you can share your specific circumstances, experiences, failures and lessons.

Or, in the case of fiction, only you will write that specific storyline or tell a story from a specific angle. Or simply tell a story in your unique voice.

YOU ARE UNIQUE!

Which means, your book probably will be too.

Therefore, no matter what it is that you want to write, providing you're not point-blank plagiarising anyone else's work, your book matters.

Your book deserves to be written and published, for the world to enjoy.

And quite frankly, who are YOU to be withholding your incredible knowledge, insights and stories from the rest of us?

By continuing to put your book on the backburner, you're not just robbing yourself of incredible opportunities. You're robbing the rest of the world.

One could argue that it's YOUR DUTY to share what you know.

To contribute to the collective of world knowledge.

And if that doesn't motivate you into action, I don't know what will!

But in all seriousness, there are some really valid reasons why you haven't written and published a book yet.

Which is why we've written THIS book.

There's a good chance, you're battling confidence to begin with – which we'll be tackling in Part 1.

You might be thinking things like …

Who am I to write a book?

I have no clue HOW to write?

I've never written anything before?

I failed my school English classes?

Or ...

I don't know enough about my topic yet.

I'm not qualified enough.

I'm not an expert enough.

I'm not experienced enough.

Hmmm. This enough thing is a downer, hey?

Thing is – you're already enough. In all aspects. If you know ANYTHING, that anything can be shared in a book.

Don't assume that everyone else in the world already knows that particular 'anything'. There's probably someone out there who wants to know it.

Plus, even if you don't think you're a fantastic or natural writer, that's ok.

We have an easy peasy writing process that you can follow, to help you get those words on that page.

We also have a few tricks that will help you 'write' it when you're not actually 'writing it' (Part 4).

Part 2 is super important as it will help you dedicate consistent time to allow you to make real progress with your book.

No writer should ever start writing without Part 3 – Planning.

And finally, we'll cover the basics of publishing your book, so you have a solid insight as to how to get your finished work 'out there' and in front of your readers.

So, keep reading. Let's dive right in.

And I can't wait to see your finished book.

How To Use This Book

You'll soon notice that this book has a lot of chapters, and many of the chapters are quite short.

You'll also notice that this entire book is quite short.

This has been done on purpose.

This book is intended to be a guidebook with easily actionable steps.

We want you to get writing and get published as quickly and as easily as possible.

We don't believe in adding in any unnecessary waffle – just the cold, hard facts so you can take action.

It should only take an hour or two to read your way through the content of this book.

Yet, the steps and the writing will inevitably take many months for you to carry out.

Therefore, refer back to this book anytime you encounter a problem or need the next step in the process.

Part 1: Creating The Confidence to Start

Chapter 1

You CAN Write a Book (Anyone Can!)

Writing a book can feel like something only a professional writer can do. Like writing is simply a skill you were born with, or you're not.

But that's just not the case. You don't need to be a GOOD writer to write a book.

In fact, you don't even need to 'write it' (more on that later).

How is that so?

Well, it's a matter of learning a solid process, to begin with.

PLUS – and here's a secret – a good editor can make just about ANY writing shine.

Trust me, NO ONE, not even the biggest and best authors, spit out a perfect book, the first time.

Sure, sometimes, it may spill out of them word perfect from the get-go.

But chances are, most of the time it won't. It will be rough. In fact, it will often be a jumbled mess.

And the finished product, isn't all them and their exact words, necessarily.

They might write the bare bones, that scrappy first draft – but it's often an editor (or 5!) who actually polishes the content up to the required standard for publishing.

It's incredibly easy to look at and read all the fabulous books out there and believe that you don't have a snowball's chance at sounding or looking that great.

But trust me when I say that even the most experienced writers and authors have a team of specialists helping them to sound that good.

In fact, many of the higher-level, more prominent authors have book coaches who help them extensively throughout the writing process. They may also even use a ghost writer (someone who writes the book for them, but makes it sound like them) and you wouldn't even know it.

As with anything, books aren't always what they seem. They are a group and team effort.

So if there's one single thing you can take away from this book, let it be this ...

Writing can be learnt.

Editors are awesome.

And anyone can write a book. Including you!

Chapter 2

Your Idea, Story & Experience IS Valid

Lots of people have an idea for a book but worry that it's not a topic that anyone will want to know about.

Or, if it's a story about themselves, that no one will be interested in them.

Yet I guarantee that you've read plenty of incredible books and stories, written by authors who felt the same way in the beginning.

Any idea and story is completely valid.

Because there is ALWAYS someone out there in the world, who wants and needs to hear it.

With so many people in the world, how could there not be?

Now, of course, this comes with a few little caveats.

This entirely depends on your PURPOSE in writing your book.

Some topics are clearly going to have larger audiences and potential readerships, than others.

If you're planning on writing a non-fiction book, you'll want to do a bit of research into your topic to make sure the right people will want it. You want to ensure your story will have 'marketability'.

This is the case IF you want to make real money out of being a fiction author anyway. If you're simply writing it for your own enjoyment and sense of achievement – it doesn't matter in the slightest if your story doesn't have mass market appeal.

If you're writing a book for positioning and growing your business, you'll want to validate that your idea is the right one to achieve your specific goals.

Here are a few ideas to help you validate your book idea:

Research on Amazon

Take a look at the type of books that are trending on Amazon, particularly within your chosen knowledge area category or genre.

This will help you gauge demand for a particular topic or area of expertise.

Don't worry about tackling a topic that's already been done before. Remember that just about everything has been done. It's all about providing your own unique perspective and voice. And finding your own angle or niche.

Search Google

Do a Google search for words around your potential book topic and name (if you've come up with one). It's a good idea to try and make sure that there aren't any books already named exactly the same. Although, if it's unavoidable, you can distinguish your title from everyone else's by crafting a unique subtitle.

Then, ask yourself these questions...

Is this something I'm passionate about?

You should be passionate and enthusiastic about your chosen topic – as this will keep you motivated, and it will come across through your writing.

If you find a topic boring, chances are, your writing will be boring too.

Is this something I know about?

You should have some existing personal expertise and experience in what you're writing about.

You don't have to know everything, as you can do some research, but it helps when you have your own personal stories around the various aspects you're teaching.

Is there an audience?

If you already know the audience you're speaking to, that's great.

If not, you may need to go hunting down your audience.

Make sure you can find your people.

- Try Facebook groups.

- Try any membership organisations or associations you're a part of.

- Try to look at what successful people in your industry or niche are successfully selling.

The more you understand the market you're wanting to position your book within, the more likely you are to be able to write the perfect book that achieves your goals.

Chapter 3

How to Cultivate Self Belief

Self-belief can be ever so tricky – and especially when it comes to writing books.

There are few things that feel quite as BOLD as saying 'I'm writing a book' and 'I want to become a published author'.

And there's literally evidence everywhere around you as to why you CANNOT write a book.

I mean how on earth could you be so silly? To think YOU could actually do this.

I bet you've probably already ran the idea past someone you know.

And I double bet, that someone has already told you that it's impossible and just can't be done. Or at least, it's so hard that it's not worth trying.

You've possibly been told:

- You have no time.

- You're not a writer.

- You're an ok writer, but not good enough to write a REAL book.

- You're not enough of an expert on your topic.

- You haven't had enough industry experience.

- You're only 25 – you're too young.

- You're over 50 – you're too old.

You're too this, not enough of that.

There's also a good chance that this is what you're telling yourself!

Guess what – that's all a load of bulldust.

Time can be made.

Anyone can learn to write (or use an alternative method to 'write').

There is no perfect age to write a book.

You can write it at ANY stage of your life, career or business.

How? Because I can just about guarantee that you know something that others haven't learnt yet.

You can share that. You can write about that.

But back to the 'evidence' thing.

You can totally CHOOSE to find all the reasons and all the evidence why you CAN'T write a book.

OR – you can absolutely CHOOSE to look and discover all of the evidence as to why you CAN.

This applies to everything in life, by the way. This is a very important life lesson.

It's a matter of making a conscious choice to focus on the CAN – and find evidence to support your belief in the CAN.

Rather, than finding the evidence of the CAN'T.

Here's something I want you to do ...

Start collecting evidence that says you CAN write a book.

Do a little research into authors who might be:

- A similar age.

- A similar industry.

- A similar background ...

And start realising that there are many, many diverse and interesting authors out there and one of them might as well be you.

After all, why not?

The BIGGEST obstacle stopping you from writing a book – is your pesky, complicated, overly emotional human brain that keeps trying to keep you small and safe.

It's a natural human tendency. We are wired to stay within our comfort zones and to seek out safety. Which is generally, the place that we already know and have mastered. Yet no good and no growth comes from listening to that inbuilt fear reaction.

If you're interested in learning about this further, please go read *The Big Leap* by Gay Hendricks.

The general gist though, is that you need to find the evidence that supports the theory that you CAN do something. You CAN write a book.

And simply decide to go for it.

No matter what.

Without excuses.

Make it happen.

Chapter 4

Take it One Step at a Time

Writing a book and getting it produced and published can appear to be really daunting at first.

The trick is though, just like with anything big you want to achieve, is to break the BIG goal, into lots of TINY steps.

You've surely heard that old adage of 'How do you eat an elephant? One step at a time.'

It's unlikely you're going to have an idea for a book, decide you're going to write it and just sit down and write the entire thing straight off the bat. I'm sorry to say that it's not going to take you two hours or be done within a week.

Writing a book within a matter of days or a week or two is definitely possible, but chances are, if this is your first book, it's going to take a fair bit longer than that.

(You also don't want to put too much pressure on yourself the first time around. Let your book unfold over at least a month or two. Don't rush!)

You're much more likely to need to do a little research, mull over the idea for a little bit, do some brainstorming around your idea and then start putting some concrete plans together.

Smart writers and book authors – in fact smart anyone(!) – PLANS FIRST.

Which is why we've written this book, to break down the process for you.

To give you the steps needed, to create a really GOOD book that WORKS.

One. Step. At. A. Time.

Part 2:
Dedicating The Time To Write

Chapter 5

Set Aside Time Consistently

Now that we've hopefully helped you to decide you CAN become an author and that you WILL get a book written, it's time to figure out HOW you're going to do this.

TRUTH – The BIGGEST thing that will determine whether or not you succeed in writing a book – is MAKING the time to do it.

You will need to ensure that you purposefully BLOCK OUT specific writing time in your calendar.

And preferably, on a regular, consistent basis.

Now, your own personal schedule will play a huge part in how MUCH time you can dedicate to book writing.

If you're juggling work, businesses, clients, kids, family – all that stuff – you may have to be prepared to write it a little bit slower.

But there are no real rules here. It's entirely up to you how you go about it.

Some writers, like myself, absolutely LOVE going away on a 'writing holiday'.

This takes you away from your daily life and routine – away from any distractions like family and work – so you have the dedicated space and time to go nuts, and get that writing done ASAP.

If you were to work all day, every day – you could well get a finished first draft pumped out in a couple of weeks.

But it may not be possible for you to do that. Taking time out from work and family can be near impossible.

Your other option is to simply choose a writing schedule that you can manage, within your daily life.

This might be:

- A day a month

- A weekend a month.

- A day per week.

- Two hours per week.

You literally just have to make a decision based on your best guess as to what's going to be consistently feasible – block it out in your calendar – and do it.

There's nothing wrong with a slow and steady approach, if that's all you can manage.

Just make sure you are consistently making progress.

You may also find that you do need to remain flexible with your schedule, depending on things that might be happening in the rest of your life or family. Or, if you're finding your initial chosen schedule just isn't working well enough for you.

Guard Your Writing Time With Your Life

It's really easy to let yourself get distracted by life's demands. And it's easy for others around you to try and disrupt your writing time.

You really do need to stay strong with your writing schedule however, or your book just will never happen.

You need to make it a priority and insist that others around you take it seriously, too.

There's no need to feel guilty about doing this, and yes, even if you are a mum, or a busy business owner with staff to manage or any other number of excuses.

If your book is important and a part of your strategic life and/or business goals, it should be a priority. At least, to some degree.

Chapter 6

Set Targets & Rewards

Keeping yourself motivated can be really tricky, as writing a book can indeed be a lengthy process.

It can feel like you're writing and writing and writing some more and never ever getting anywhere.

The trick to combat this 'never-ending' feeling is to set yourself some targets – and then reward yourself when you reach them.

A target, for example, might be to write 3,000 words each week.

Then, you might pick something to reward yourself with when you reach that target.

Maybe it's a meal out with your partner or a movie night.

Maybe it's a Friday afternoon walk down to the beach.

Maybe it's a bar of special chocolate you enjoy.

It can be anything!

Anything that means something to you.

But setting targets and picking a reward for meeting them – IF you KEEP them – will help keep you and your book writing on track.

There is a catch here though!

If you set the wrong target, it won't work.

You need to ensure you're not aiming too small, so that you're not slowing down your potential progress. You don't want to go too easy on yourself!

And you need to ensure you're not aiming too unrealistically BIG, or you'll just get disheartened or discouraged.

In order to set a GOOD target there's a few ways you can go about it.

Firstly, you can set yourself a word goal for your entire book – and a timeframe in which you would like to have it finished.

Then, you can simply divide your word count goal by the timeframe in either months or weeks (or both!) – to get the number of words you need to write each week or each month.

Alternatively, you might like to test yourself a little by writing as much as you can for an hour – checking your word count, and then multiply that by the number of hours you want to dedicate to your book each week.

Or, if you prefer, you could work on your book for a week as per your chosen schedule, then add up the number of words you reach – add 500 or 1000 words and that's your target.

If you're really pig-headed and determined to smash your book writing out quickly though, you might just set yourself a lofty target of say 10,000 words per week and do whatever it takes to make that happen.

Chapter 7

Get Accountability

Self-motivation for big projects like this doesn't always happen easily.

When we're just answering to ourselves, it's far too easy to let ourselves down, with promises of doing better tomorrow or next week.

Finding someone else to keep you accountable and on track is often super necessary.

Do you have a:

- best friend
- business buddy

- writing group

- your mum or dad

- your partner

- an older child?

It doesn't really matter who it is, so long as it's someone who can check in with you once a week or once a month – to tap you on the shoulder and ask whether you've met your writing targets?

If so, get them lined up as soon as you can.

If you don't have anyone who's keen to take on this role – or if they just aren't 'pushy' enough to keep you on track – there are plenty of professional book coaches who can offer you support and accountability. Sometimes this is individual or one to one, other times you can save some money and join a smaller group coaching program.

Either way – hiring a coach is a great investment to make if it actually helps you to get your book finished.

We all need that little bit of 'butt-kicking' to keep us on track.

Enlist some outside support, to keep your book progressing.

Part 3: Planning Out Your Book

Chapter 8

The Why, What, How and Who

Purpose

It's important to make sure you set a very clear purpose for your book, from the very beginning.

This is MOST important if you're writing a non-fiction book to help position yourself and/or your business.

Otherwise, you're just stabbing in the dark and hoping for the best.

Start by asking ...

WHY – do I want to write a book? What's the motivation?

WHAT – will it prove or help me achieve?

HOW – will I use it to advance by profile?

WHO – will want to read it?

Clearly, if you're writing a fictional story, this isn't quite as important.

However, you'll still want to understand your intended audience and what they want and need.

As with anything in life – always start with the end goal in mind.

Audience

When looking at your potential audience – you'll need to know these types of things:

- Age

- Location

- Living Conditions

- Lifestyle

- Motivations

- Education Level

- Employment Status

You'll also need to know:

- What problems do they have?

- How can your book solve those problems?

- What do they want?

- What do they need?

- What motivates them?

- What do they do for fun?

None of these are definitive lists, but they should give you a bit of an idea.

When you get clear on your audience, you can then make sure your truly book delivers – for your audience and for yourself.

Types & Genres of Books

There are many different types of books. You may choose to pick one – or a combination of a few, if that's more appropriate.

We've put together some basic lists, but these are not extensive – they are just a starting point.

Fiction

- Fantasy

- Science Fiction

- Action

- Mystery

- Crime

- Horror

- Thriller

- Romance

- Feel Good

Non-Fiction

- Memoir

- Biography

- Instructional

- Factual

- Historical

- Real Life Stories & Lessons

- Advice

- Inspirational

Children's

- Baby & Toddler

- Pre-Primary

- Primary School/Junior

- Secondary School/Young Adult

Chapter 9

Choosing Your Topic & Title

Topics

There's a good chance that if you're doing this course, you already have an idea for your book topic – or the basic gist of a storyline.

However, it's important to really hone in on your idea to make sure you're being really specific.

Non-Fiction

While yes, you can write a general 'plant' book or a top-level overview of a massive topic – that can be fine.

It's often easier and neater and more effective to narrow down your focus.

Particularly with a business positioning book, you'll want your topic to be slightly more narrowed down or 'niche' to help you stand out AND to help your audience with a specific problem.

Therefore, instead of writing about the entire topic of 'Marketing' – you might choose something you want to specialise in or be known for such as 'Network Marketing' or 'Relationship Marketing'.

Do a little brainstorming, particularly if you have multiple topics or multiple angles that you think you could write about.

Jot all of them down, then see if you can put some structure around each.

Remember though, this is just top-level thinking to clarify your topic and idea and to choose your exact angle.

Hint: The very best non-fiction books focus on a particular challenge or problem that a specific audience tends to encounter – and then have the book describe a solution to solve that problem for that type of person.

Fiction

Here's a good place to define your story in a little more detail.

You might like to jot down:

- Main theme

- Main characters

- Secondary characters

- Conflict

- How the conflict is resolved

- Outcomes

Not a definitive list, but a start.

Titles

Titles are really tricky to come up with and to get right.

And often, it's actually easier to write the entire book first, before deciding on the title.

It's good to get a few ideas down on paper though, to help give you a bit of a guideline to work towards.

Create a 'working title' at the very least. You can then refine it with an editor or publishers' assistance, once the entire book is complete.

Options:

- Use 1 Word – tend to be quite popular.

- Use 2 or 3 Words – also popular.

- Use a longer sentence.

Keep in mind that a good title:

- Generates intrigue

- Piques interest

- Gives an insight into the topic or story.

A title can be as descriptive or as creative as you like – after all, it's your book and your creative license.

It is good to keep in mind though what words you use in comparison to what a reader might search for on Google or Amazon. Or even a library catalogue for that matter.

Do a bit of research on Amazon to see what other titles authors have used.

You can also use a shorter, more creative or impact-driven main title, and then use a more descriptive or explanatory sub-title that helps your reader and includes a few specific keywords.

Chapter 10

Chapter &
Content
Planning

This is where we create an outline or the structure of your book content.

The best way I find to do this, is to simply brainstorm and brain dump every single thing you can possibly think of, around your chosen book topic.

Did you ever do a mind map at school?

That's essentially what we're after.

You can draw and write it by hand – or you can just type dot points on your computer. Whichever works best for you.

Then, it's a matter of grouping pieces of information into chapters and sub-topics.

Step 1: Brainstorm everything

Get it all down on the page, everything you can think of related to your topic.

Don't moderate yourself.

Spit it ALL out.

Step 2: Review and group

See if you can pick out any common themes running through your dot points.

Group them together, and these can become your chapters.

You may have a set process you're taking people through for example and each step of your process would then become a chapter.

Step 3: Name your chapters (if you can)

Now that you have some themes – that are becoming chapters – you can give them a chapter name.

You don't have to do this, but it's a good idea as it provides both you the guidance to write them – and the reader an insight into what each chapter contains.

Just like your book title, these can be plain descriptive headings or something a little more creative. Don't be afraid to infuse some of your personality or a bit of fun into them. Unless you're writing a scientific paper, they don't necessarily have to be 'formal' or dry.

Step 4: Map pieces of information under each chapter

Once you have your chapters mapped out, it's time to match up all the information, facts, quotes, figures and statements you brainstormed, under the appropriate one.

This will give you your chapter outlines.

For Example:

Introduction

Chapter 1: [Title]

- Idea 1

- Idea 2

- Idea 3

Chapter 2: [Title]

- Quote

- Story

- Teach

- Next Steps

- Transition to Next Chapter

And so on.

Part 4: Writing Your Book

Chapter 11

Writing Your First Draft

There is a golden rule that you must learn when writing your first draft.

YOUR FIRST DRAFT IS SUPPOSED TO BE RIDICULOUSLY ROUGH!

The trick to great writing – and getting words on the page as quickly as possible – is to simply spit it all out, any way it comes.

You MUST NOT moderate yourself, in any way.

Just put the thoughts inside your head, down on the page.

If everything comes out a complete jumble, that's ok.

You can and WILL refine it later.

That's precisely what the editing process is for.

Where to Start

So, you have your chapters and your content plan, as per the planning section.

The idea now, is to simply start writing about each of the topics you listed in your plan, under each chapter.

If you need to do any research for any of the sections, you can do that as you go and work it into your content.

OR – if it helps, do the research for each of the sections – dump it on the page, and then write each section (and delete the raw research after).

It's also up to you whether you write sequentially, from start to finish.

Some writers like to start with the introduction, move on to Chapter 1, then Chapter 2 etc.

Sometimes writing the introduction first can help set the scene for your creative brain, making the rest easier.

But quite often, I like to write the individual chapters and sections first and leave the introduction and conclusion until last.

It can be easier at times to get all the body content written, so you can then write the introduction once you know the full scope of your book.

But it really is a personal choice.

Beware the Messy Middle

The 'Messy Middle' is when you hit those middle parts of your book. The initial motivation and enthusiasm generally starts to wear off by this point – and yet, there is still so much more to write.

This is where you can feel very unmotivated and overwhelmed.

The only thing you can do here is to understand what it is and why – accept that it's normal – and keep pushing yourself through it.

Keep plodding, keep on writing and you'll get there.

The end will keep getting closer and closer.

Where to Finish

You can finish your book or story anywhere you desire.

There is a caveat though, in that you need to make sure you don't continue to waffle or go off track with your writing.

Your book will need a clear finish point. And you need to remember to stick to your original plan (unless you have a brain wave that really does add more value to your book content!) – and to stay very focused on your book's purpose.

If you're writing a story, you'll want to craft a strong finish to your storyline to ensure it wraps up everything that the characters have gone through – but perhaps leaves a little intrigue for later, just in case you're planning a sequel.

For a non-fiction, factual book, it's great to leave readers with an overview of what they've learnt and perhaps an inspiring story that helps to motivate them to take action from the information they've gained.

You'll also want a gentle 'call to action' to point people towards their next step with you, whether it's to check out your website or to download a free resource.

Chapter 12

Banish Writer's Block

Experiencing 'writer's block' can be incredibly frustrating.

Even the most experienced writers hit this wall from time to time.

It's not something you should be fearing, however.

There are ways to get around it. And when you go to the effort of planning out your book thoroughly before you start, you'll possibly find that you don't encounter it at all.

Particularly, if you keep the following in mind.

Remain Flexible

I quite often find that I don't write sequentially from start to finish.

In fact, I didn't write this book in order either, from chapter 1, chapter 2, etc.

I find that my brain sometimes needs to jump around a topic, depending on where it's feeling inspired at the time.

So, if I'm finding chapter 2 too hard to write – I might skip a few chapters ahead and write chapter 5 first, instead.

I quite often begin by writing the easiest sections of content first, to get those creative juices firing – and build some momentum – before tackling the slightly harder ones.

Don't get stuck thinking you have to do this writing thing perfectly – or that there are any set rules.

Kick Perfection to the Curb

It's easy to get stuck in the mindset of HAVING to find the PERFECT words ALL of the time.

But usually, something is enough.

It's really important to not get hung up about things for the first draft.

You can get technical and more creative later.

Change Writing Locations

Sometimes, you just need a change of environment or scenery.

Take your laptop outside, down to the local park or to the beach.

Maybe you need a hotel room for a weekend.

Or just sit outside on the balcony, rather than at your desk.

A change of environment can really refresh your mental juices and spark creativity and enthusiasm again.

Make a Solid Routine

It might seem counterintuitive to creativity, to have a routine around your writing – but it can actually help.

Whether you're doing an hour a day, or 3 hours on a Sunday afternoon – when you create a routine and train your brain, you'll often find things start to happen more easily.

Go Have Some Fun

To enhance your mood – sometimes you just need to go do something really silly or light-hearted.

If you have kids – go play with them.

Bounce on the trampoline. Run around the backyard with the dog. Ride a horse.

Do some Lego. Or a jigsaw puzzle. Chase your kids on their bikes.

Take a Break

Give writing a temporary rest and go do something else.

Go for a brisk walk in the fresh air to give your brain a rest and get the endorphins flowing.

If necessary, leave it for a day.

Just be careful here. While taking a break can help – you don't want to get stuck in a loop of 'taking a break' and then never getting anything done.

So, it's always a very temporary break.

Chapter 13

Alternative Ways of 'Writing'

Most of us assume that writing must physically happen in the 'traditional' way.

That is – you sit down at the computer – and type away on a keyboard, to make the words appear on the screen.

That's how I do it as a professional writer – yes.

But it's not the only way!

Here are some other ways ...

Speak Your Book

Did you know that many authors in fact SPEAK their book content?

This is really handy if you're a natural talker, speaker or presenter – as you can literally talk your content into a recording device, and then get it transcribed onto paper.

Hey presto, words on the page.

Hire a Ghost Writer

You can actually hire a ghost writer to write your book for you – on your behalf.

And yes, you can still put your name as the author. And yes, a good ghost writer can make it sound exactly like you.

Now, this is generally incredibly expensive, as it's quite a complex process for a ghost writer to extract all the knowledge and insights from your head, and then put it into the right words that sound like you.

But it certainly can be done and it's a great option if you have the budget, but limited time.

Do Bits of Everything

Sometimes, you just need to mix things up.

Perhaps there are some chapters where you feel like simply tapping away on a keyboard.

And maybe there's others where you can't be bothered, and it's easier to just say it into a recording device.

There are no rules.

Get those words on to the page anyway you possibly can.

Keep a Recording Device Handy

It's also wise to note that it's often when you're NOT writing or even thinking about writing, that you'll have the best ideas.

Sometimes you'll literally get a string of words or the perfect paragraph hit you, while you're in the shower, driving the car or walking the dog.

Instead of trying to remember your thoughts until you can get home to write it down ...

And risk forgetting the entire thing ...

Keep a recording device handy so you can simply talk it in – and then write it out when you can.

Nothing is more annoying than thinking of an idea or something really clever – and then forgetting it the moment you sit down in front of the computer.

If all else fails – I love Evernote on my mobile phone.

It's perfect for jotting things down when I suddenly have brain waves while trying to get to sleep!

Collaborative Books

If writing an entire book by yourself feels way too hard for where you're at right now, contributing a chapter (or two) to a collaborative book or anthology can be a really great place to start.

The idea is that there's a central organiser who coordinates the book project, plus somewhere between 8 and 30 authors who band together to each write a single chapter of the book.

A full book can be upwards of 60,000 words, whereas a single chapter can be around 3000 – 4000 words. A significant reduction in your effort.

Different collaborative books or anthologies have different purposes, but the main one tends to be business books.

Writing and getting published has fantastic benefits for business owners, and by contributing to a collaborative book, you're both networking and getting to know the other authors – but you also get in front of their audiences.

See, when all the other authors promote the book to their audiences, their audience then ends up reading your chapter and getting to know you. And likewise, you're helping other business owners by putting the book in front of your audience.

The other benefits to starting out with a collaborative book, is that the entire book production and publishing process is handled for you – therefore it's easier. But it also means you can learn the writing and publishing process on a much smaller scale and then replicate the same process for your first full book you author and publish.

Therefore, if you ever see the opportunities out there, particularly if the organiser has a large audience and access to a good publisher, don't hesitate. They are very worthwhile.

If this is something that interests you, and you're a rural, regional or remote business owner, we run our own collaborative book projects at The Rural Publishing Company. Feel free to get in touch if you'd like to be involved.

Part 5: Editing

Chapter 14

Self-Editing

Hooray! You have your rough first draft!

Now, it's time to add the magic, by self-editing your work.

Note: If you don't want to self-edit, you absolutely don't have to. You can simply pay a professional editor (see next video) to handle things from here.

However, I like to do this stage, to make sure I'm saying everything I want to say – and the way I want to say it.

It's also amazing just how much you'll pick up on – and end up ADDING to your chapters, when you do this.

The Process

With fresh eyes, and taking it section by section, or chapter by chapter, re-read what you've written – and start fixing it up.

You need to be looking for the immediately obvious:

- Sentence construction

- Whether everything makes sense and ties together

- Spelling

- Grammar

- Too long sentences

- Missing facts

- Does your content need an extra quote/sentence/paragraph?

- Have you explained each concept fully?

- Have you got unnecessary words?

- Have you randomly switched between active and passive voice?

- Have you used a 'fancy' or too technical word? Can you simplify?

Tools to Help

There are actually quite a few tools out there that can help you to edit your work.

The simplest is Microsoft Word or Google Documents. In fact, I often find that Google Docs offers better editing suggestions, so it does pay to transfer things from Word to Google to help you.

Otherwise, there is specific writing software out there too. You may find yourself more comfortable with some of these, but often they come at a cost, and I have never found them necessary.

You may like to take a look at:

- Scrivener

- ProWritingAid

- Freedom

- Novel Factory.

Otherwise, in terms of editing, these two tools are really valuable to have up your sleeve.

Grammarly - https://www.grammarly.com/

This is brilliant at guiding you as you write. It checks your spelling and grammar, but also makes suggestions on style and tone.

Hemingway - https://hemingwayapp.com/

This helps you with your readability. It ranks your content at an education level and tells you how to make it more easily understood.

Chapter 15

Professional Editing

Professional editing is pretty much ALWAYS needed for any book.

And there are two approaches.

One, is to use a general book editor. So, that's one person who does one comprehensive edit.

The other option is to use a range of specialist editors.

Because there are actually different TYPES of editing and editors.

Let's take a look.

Developmental Editor

This is all about the big picture ideas in your book.

A Developmental Editor might advise on:

- Structure

- Plot

- Characters

- Information

Content Editor

A Content Editor goes a little bit further and looks at:

- Style

- Flow

- Consistency

- Tone

- Re-Organises Information.

Line Editor

Line Editors look at the content line by line, to:

- Tighten Sentences

- Shorten Paragraphs

- Improve Readability.

Copy Editor

This gets in to the nitty gritty of:

- Grammar

- Spelling

- Readability

Basically, everything in more detail.

Phew! That's a lot, hey?

Whether you choose to go for a more general editor – and a single person – or, to go through the more complex process of multiple specialist editors, is entirely up to you.

Clearly, you're likely to get a better result by using a range of specialists, particularly for a longer fiction book or a more complex non-fiction book.

However, so long as you get a GOOD general editor, that's obviously a cheaper and quicker option, and can work just as well.

For example: My book *Rural Business Women*, just used a single general editor, and it came out absolutely perfect.

It just depends on how technical you want to get.

Chapter 16

Final Proofreading

Hurrah! Now we're really up to the final step.

Final proofreading is absolutely essential, to make sure that absolutely NOTHING has slipped through the cracks.

You want to make sure that every little full stop, capital letter, spelling error has been picked up.

Now, this can be done both after editing within the manuscript (or within your Word Document etc.).

But also, needs to be done once your manuscript has been typeset or laid out in its final print form.

Typesetting or internal layout should ideally be completed by a professional, who knows how to do this. Getting margins, headings, page numbers etc. all correct so that it both looks good and prints correctly is really critical to providing a good reader experience.

You don't want words hidden in the folds etc.!

So, both BEFORE typesetting takes place AND AFTER – you should be proofreading.

Ideally – you'll do both proofreads and so will a professional proofreader, with fresh eager eyes.

This will reduce the chance of any mistakes, once you go to print.

Part 6: Publishing Your Book

Chapter 17

Publishing Methods

Congratulations! This is where you can go out and celebrate your achievements. Make sure you do something to mark the occasion as it really is something to be proud of.

However, the job clearly isn't done yet.

Now that you have a finished manuscript it's time for the publishing process to begin.

You'll now need:

- A cover design

- Internal images

- Internal layout design/typesetting (if you haven't

already)

- A blurb

- A foreword, references, dedication etc. (if desired).

- An ISBN for each version of your book

- A barcode for print

- To get your final files produced

- To upload your files for print on demand and global distribution

- To print your first print copies

- To upload your eBook to Amazon (if desired)

- And finally – to start promoting and selling!

There's certainly a lot to decide on and get done. And it's not an easy process if you're a first timer.

When it comes to publishing, you have three main options.

Do-It-Yourself Self-Publishing

This is where you handle the entire process, from start to finish, yourself. That means finding a cover designer, a typesetter, an editor, a proof reader and trying to figure out distribution and platforms such as Amazon yourself.

It does however give you ALL the control in the world over how your finished book turns out. And, you of course keep all the legal rights to your work AND keep 100% of your book sale profits (minus any platform commissions and the print cost where applicable). This generally works out to be about $5 to $8 per copy in profit (based off a $29.95 retail price), which is considered to be quite good.

This is how I first began when I published my first book. I basically 'Googled' all the steps, and through a lot of trial and error, managed to do it all myself.

But believe me when I say, I wasted so many hours trying to figure things out and it was not straight forward. It literally drove me insane.

So while yes, DIY self-publishing is very possible, it's not easy and it's incredibly time consuming.

Traditional Publishing

Traditional publishers can be really tricky to get signed up with, as they will only take on higher profile authors or people who already have a large audience online. This is to make sure that they can make enough money from your work. They will also only accept submissions via an agent – and they will only take on a very select range of topic or story ideas.

Generally, they may pay you an advance on your royalties, which essentially means you're getting paid in advance to write your book. That sounds appealing, right? However, these are your future predicted book sale commission proceeds – you're simply getting them paid in advance. Traditionally, an advance might have been $10,000 to $20,000. However, these days, the amounts are getting much smaller ($2,000 to $5,000 if you're lucky) and many authors don't get anything at all. Particularly, if you're a new author.

On the flip side however, you'll only be making around $1 to $2 per book in book sale profits. The publisher (and your agent) keeps the rest. They also tend to own the legal rights to your work – which means as soon as you hand your manuscript over – they make all the decisions regarding things such as cover design and marketing. You get a very limited say on how your book is produced.

Assisted or Supported Self-Publishing

This is where you utilise the services of a supported self-publishing company. It's basically the best of both worlds – where you get the expertise and support of a professional team who handle everything for you, yet you still keep the rights to your work, control how your book is put together and keep 100% of your book sale profits (minus print costs and platform commissions).

This means you don't need to worry about finding a cover designer, a typesetter or an editor. And you don't need to try and navigate producing your digital and print book files, or distribution or uploading it to Amazon etc. This sort of publisher can do it all for you, for a set fee.

The other advantage is that you can simply wake up one morning and DECIDE to become an author and to get published. You do not need to pitch your book ideas to agents or publishers or wait YEARS for a publisher to choose you and your manuscript.

You can simply go out and get it done.

In fact, often, many high-profile authors begin this way. They start by using a supported self-publishing service and once their book starts gaining momentum and becoming successful – a traditional publishing house will sometimes offer them a contract.

Clearly, this option does require you, as the author, to pay for these publishing services upfront (or via a payment plan). However, long-term, when you're earning higher sales commissions, it actually works out to be more profitable ...

Traditional Advance (They Pay You) = $5,000

Royalties Per Book = $1

You would need to achieve 5,000 book sales before seeing another cent.

Pay a Supported Self-Publisher = $5,000

Royalties Per Book = $5

You only need to sell 1,000 books to recoup your costs (anything else is profit).

If you sell 5,000 copies = you make $25,000 profit.

It's sure interesting when you do the maths.

If you're looking for a good supported self-publishing company, particularly if you're a rural, regional or remote author – we can certainly help you out at The Rural Publishing Company.

You will still need to submit your manuscript to us before we offer you a contract, as we do have set requirements and quality standards you will need to meet.

Chapter 18

ISBN's & Barcodes

ISBN's

According to Thorpe-Bowker Australia...

"The ISBN is a unique identifier for a book or other book-like product (such as an audiobook) that specifies its format, edition, and publisher.

There are many reasons to purchase an ISBN for your title, including:

- *An ISBN improves the likelihood your book will be found and purchased*

- *An ISBN links to essential information about your*

book

- *An ISBN enables more efficient marketing and distribution of your title*

- *Most retailers require ISBNs*

- *An ISBN helps you collect and analyse book sales data*

- *An ISBN ensures your book's information will be stored in the Books In Print database*

- *Books In Print is consulted by publishers, retailers and libraries around the world when searching for title information."*

So basically, if you want to publish a book the RIGHT way and have it taken seriously – you need one.

And you need one for each format you publish your book in.

So, you will at a minimum need TWO ISBN's – one for your print version, one for your eBook version.

If you wish to publish as an audiobook – you will need a third for that too.

The place you need to go to get them is clearly Thorpe-Bowker Australia.

These guys are the central organisation who administer and sell ISBN's.

Simply go here (this link will be in the accompanying material):

https://www.myidentifiers.com.au/identify-protect-your-book/isbn/buy-isbn

Or just type ISBN into Google.

You can buy an ISBN number individually – or in packs.

Considering buying 2 ISBN's is the same price as their 10-Pack – I highly recommend the 10-Pack, as you never know when you might need the extras. A second and third book perhaps?

(Many authors who write their first book, do tend to get addicted, so be warned.)

Once you have purchased your ISBN numbers – you will get a login account with Thorpe-Bowker – so you can assign them to your book versions. Do this carefully!

HUGE HINT: You can also buy a pack of 10 ISBN numbers and 1 barcode – and there are numerous other high value packages on offer.

See the next section on barcodes ...

Barcodes

Clearly, a barcode is that little scannable image and code on products, and on the back of books.

And it needs to be formulated from your ISBN once you assign your publication.

The barcode then needs to be placed within your back cover design.

Again, you can purchase these through Thorpe-Bowker Australia.

As mentioned in the previous lesson – barcodes can be purchased in a pack, alongside your ISBN's, at a cheaper rate. This is well worth doing.

You will only need one barcode for your print book, however.

Chapter 19

Blurbs, Forewords, References & More

Blurbs

Alongside your actual manuscript of your book content –
you will need a blurb or a summary, to go on your back cover.

This is not always easy to write and it's very necessary to get
RIGHT.

If you struggle to do it yourself, there's no harm in asking a writer to do it for you. It's not expensive and worth the effort to have it written well.

Besides the front cover, your blurb is the second most important thing to get right, so people are drawn to reading and purchasing your book.

It should contain an overview of the book and provide a clear insight into its contents.

Yet, it should also act as a 'sales piece' that hooks and draws people in. A little sales psychology, mystery and intrigue is a great idea.

Forewords

A foreword is not necessary for your book, but many people like to have them.

A foreword is written by someone else, to help introduce you and your topic and what the book is about.

Often, it's great if it can be someone with a high profile, who helps to position you as an expert and gives your book more authority.

If you'd like to incorporate one, make sure you approach your chosen person well in advance, to give them time to write it.

References

If you have quoted material from other publications and sources, you will need a reference list at the back of your book.

This helps the reader with their 'further reading' should they feel compelled to dive into a topic that little bit more.

But it also makes sure that you're not plagiarising anyone else's thoughts or ideas.

Referencing correctly is complicated, so again, seeking help is best if you're unsure.

Acknowledgements

You may also like to publish some acknowledgments in your book of anyone who has helped you in your book writing, business or life journey.

These are entirely up to you and can be nice to include.

Dedications

Again, dedications are not necessary, but you may like to have a dedication at the beginning of your book, to someone who has inspired you.

Chapter 20

Cover Design

Your cover design is one of the most critical parts of your book (besides the writing and editing!), that you need to get right.

Your cover is what sells your book.

It is what attracts a reader's eye and attention as they scan the shelves at their local bookstore or as they scroll through Amazon.

There are multiple options with covers.

You can:

- Use a headshot of yourself

- Use words and colours only

- Use a combination of your title words and an image

– whether it's in a formal style or a more modern, casual look.

I strongly suggest you start by researching other book covers in your industry and area of expertise.

And I also strongly recommend you look at other covers that are in the Best Sellers lists on Amazon.

This will give you an idea of what is currently trending, what you like, what you don't like and provide you with an idea around the style you would like.

Imagery really does help to set up those vital first impressions with readers and journalists – so every little element on your front cover page needs to be there for a reason.

It needs to make a potential reader connect and FEEL something about the content of the book.

Unless you are a super-duper graphic designer yourself – I highly recommend outsourcing this part of the process to a professional.

Even if that means you roughly put together a concept, and find an affordable book cover designer on Fiverr. If you don't have much budget, that might be your best bet.

If you can, you can locate a professional, locally based designer who has, preferably, experience with book cover design.

It is quite a fine art and a specialist area of expertise – to make sure it's all produced in the right formats and at the right sizes etc.

Hint: A common 'trim size' for non-fiction is 6 inches by 9 inches (229mm x 152mm). Or 5.5 inches by 8.5 inches for fiction.

But I highly recommend checking out this article for further advice on this: https://www.ingramspark.com/blog/picking-a-popular-trim-size-for-your-book.

Chapter 21

Internal Layout

This is where you lay out the content of your book on the page.

As with designing your book cover, it's important to know precisely how to do this, for the size of the book you wish to print, to ensure a solid reader experience.

No ones to see chopped off words or messy heading formatting etc.

Internal layout can be done in Microsoft Word, providing you know how. You will need to set elements such as page margins, page breaks, headers and footers.

And producing reflowable eBook files can be a nightmare.

That's why we use industry-specific typesetting software that produces all the correct files. This tends to give the best results for both print and eBook formats.

If your budget is limited and you are self-publishing, you may be able to find providers on Fiverr who can do this for you.

Just keep in mind, with lower quality providers, you will need to check their work and go over your entire book with a fine-toothed comb.

Despite the fact that they may simply be 'copying and pasting' or simply formatting a document – errors can easily occur, and things can get lost in translation.

Make sure you include your publishing, edition and any disclaimer information at the front in the correct format, that your table of contents is correct and that all your chapter headings and page numbers line up.

Internal layout is particularly important if you plan on printing copies of your book. You'll want to create the best reader experience possible and produce a nice, quality end result.

So, this is definitely an area where you don't want to skimp.

Chapter 22

File Production

This is going to be a very short lesson, as this can either be incredibly easy or ridiculously difficult. Fun, hey!

Chances are though, if you get someone to help you with your internal layout and cover design – they may be able to also assist you with putting the correct files together.

But if not, seek out someone who can.

Here is what you need in basic terms:

eBook – Internals should be an EPUB file, cover file (front cover only) should be a JPEG file.

Print – Internals and cover should be in PDF format. You will also need a spine and back cover.

Rather than trying to take you through all the requirements here, IngramSpark has some really useful articles to help you.

https://www.ingramspark.com/blog/file-requirements-for-print-books

https://www.ingramspark.com/blog/file-requirements-for-e books

Chapter 23

Print on Demand & Global Distribution (IngramSpark)

Here is the exciting part. The bit where we actually start uploading and feeding your magnificent new book, out, into the world.

And the secret to this bit – is IngramSpark.

This is the company who both prints and distributes your book globally.

You simply upload the files to their system – and they feed it all out.

But despite me saying 'simply' and it does SOUND simple, it can be a tricky process to navigate for first timers.

Now, we could have walked you through the entire process, but that seems pretty pointless, when IngramSpark has their own resources that are far better than ours could be.

So, here are your links to what you need to know:

https://www.ingramspark.com/blog/book-distribution-with-ingramspark

https://www.ingramspark.com/how-to-self-publish-a-book

https://www.ingramspark.com/plan-your-book/ebooks

https://www.ingramspark.com/plan-your-book/print/print-on-demand

Amazon

When you use IngramSpark for both your print on demand and distribution, they automatically feed out your eBook to Amazon, along with Booktopia and lots of others.

Which, you could consider your job done at that point.

However! I have always found it much easier to upload directly to Amazon, as doing so gives you much more control over how it appears on Amazon – and it also gives you access to Amazon's promotional features.

It's worth the effort.

Generally, it's a good idea to upload your eBook to IngramSpark first, let that get approved and go live – and wait until your eBook starts showing on Amazon FIRST.

THEN – you can go in and upload your eBook to Amazon using their KDP system.

Note: I have found that Amazon is really quite smart, in that once you upload directly to them, they match it up with the record they have already, via IngramSpark.

They then merge the two but display the details you've provided directly to them.

It's wise to note, particularly for us Aussies, that IngramSpark generally has the correct eBook pricing, but when Amazon grabs those details, they often put a percentage mark-up on them.

When you then go and upload directly – your proper pricing shows.

So, keep that in mind. Our book (*Rural Business Women*) came across from IngramSpark to Amazon, with a $10.34 price, when we had specified $9.99.

When we uploaded it directly, with the right price, that's what it showed.

Chapter 24

Printing (On Demand)

The beauty of publishing through IngramSpark yourself, is that you're in complete control of how many books you order, at any one time.

With a traditional publishing model, authors used to get completely stuck with a set number of copies – that they often didn't know how to sell.

In this case – you're paying cost or print price for each copy of the book you order, but you can literally order one copy at a time, if you wish.

I don't recommend that though.

You'll find that ordering 5+ books at a time is a better idea, due to how the pricing works out – both with the cost price per book and the shipping.

It's also handy that IngramSpark is set up so that it automatically calculates a quote online, and you can keep fiddling with that quote, until you're happy with the quantities and options.

The cost or print price of your books will depend greatly on the number of words and pages you have.

As an example, our book *Rural Business Women* is 300 pages, and costs between $10 - $14 per copy.

Make sure you utilise IngramSpark's great calculator tools on their website, as you can get a rough estimate for the book you want to write before having it finished or uploaded on to their system.

Conclusion

There's lots to consider when planning, writing and publishing a book. It can certainly be a very daunting idea to contemplate, let alone actually navigate and complete.

Yet, I want to really encourage you to give a book a red-hot go. Particularly, if you're a regional business owner looking to get ahead. Books are such a fantastic positioning tool when produced and used in the right ways. The return on your investment is usually immediate and rather mind-blowing.

Opportunities will open up for you left, right and centre the second you announce your book and yourself as a published author.

But don't think it's as easy as writing any old book and hoping for the sales to come pouring in. You need to approach a business positioning book with a tonne of clever strategy to ensure you get the right results.

However, even if you're wanting to write for pleasure and personal satisfaction – or even if it's to leave a legacy to your family or the world – it's still such a valid and wonderful pursuit.

Books are important. They stand the test of time and are treasured forever.

Don't let a lack of confidence or any other obstacle stand in your way. After all, we only live once and its up to us to make the most of it and leave our own little mark.

If you need some writing or publishing advice, please don't hesitate to reach out to us at The Rural Publishing Company. We're dedicated to supporting and empowering authors to get their work finished and out into the world.

We're always happy to look at manuscripts, finished or not, at no charge, for anyone who would like some feedback.

Plus, we have our Rural Author's Club, a low-cost online membership that provides courses, templates and support.

Finally, we wish you and your new book the greatest of luck!

We'd love to hear how you get on, so please send us a link to your published book when it's finished. We'd love to help promote you.

Thank you!

Sarah Walkerden

The Rural Publishing Company
theruralpublishingcompany.com.au
hello@theruralpublishingcompany.com.au

About the Author

Sarah Walkerden

Sarah Walkerden is the founder of The Rural Publishing Company, a pioneering publishing house dedicated to helping rural, regional and remote Australians turn their stories and expertise into books that make an impact.

A passionate advocate for amplifying rural voices, Sarah knows first-hand the unique challenges – and strengths – that come with running a business and writing a book outside the city. With a background in writing, publishing and entrepreneurship, she created The Rural Publishing Company to provide authors with the support, clarity and professional guidance they need to publish with confidence – without falling into the traps of vanity presses or overwhelm.

Through workshops, coaching and supported self-publishing packages, Sarah empowers authors to not only publish their books but also use them as powerful tools to grow their businesses, boost credibility and share their stories far beyond their local towns.

Her vision is simple but bold: to help rural authors shine, one book at a time.

Credentials & Accolades:

- Multi award-winning copywriter

- Best-selling author of *Rural Business Women*

- Featured in local and national media

- Bachelor of Technology (Interactive Multimedia)

- Certified Practising Marketer (CPM) with the Australian Marketing Institute

Sarah Walkerden

The Rural Publishing Company
Website: https://theruralpublishingcompany.com.au

www.ingramcontent.com/pod-product-compliance
Lightning Source LLC
Chambersburg PA
CBHW072146020426
42334CB00018B/1900